CITIES OF THE WORLD

TORONTO

BY BARBARA RADCLIFFE ROGERS AND STILLMAN D. ROGERS

CHILDREN'S PRESS®
A Division of Grolier Publishing
New York London Hong Kong Sydney
Danbury, Connecticut

The authors would like to thank Candee Treadway and Ralph Johansen of the Canadian Consulate in Boston, fellow travel writer Ann Carroll Burgess, and Phyllis, Len, Paul, and Colin Vernon, who first showed us Toronto.

CONSULTANT

Linda Cornwell
Coordinator of School Quality and Professional Improvement
Indiana State Teachers Association

Project Editor: Downing Publishing Services
Design Director: Karen Kohn & Associates, Ltd.
Photo Researcher: Jan Izzo

Library of Congress Cataloging-in-Publication Data
Rogers, Barbara Radcliffe.
    Toronto / by Barbara Radcliffe Rogers and Stillman D. Rogers.
        p. cm. — (Cities of the world)
    Includes bibliographical references and index.
    Summary: Describes the history, culture, points of interest, and people of Toronto, Canada's largest city, situated on the north shore of Lake Ontario.
    ISBN 0-516-22034-9 (lib. bdg.)   0-516-27169-5 (pbk.)
    1. Toronto (Ont.)—Juvenile literature. [1. Toronto (Ont.)] I. Rogers, Stillman, 1939- II. Title. III. Cities of the world (New York, N.Y.)
F1059.5.T684 R64   2000
9711.3'541—dc21
                                00-024027

GROLIER
PUBLISHING

TABLE OF CONTENTS

WATER

Toronto rises from the shore of Lake Ontario, one of the five Great Lakes. The land around the city is so low and flat that its tall buildings seem to float on the water. When the sun shines on it, the city sparkles and gleams, reflecting in the lake like a mirage. The tall, futuristic needle shape of the CN Tower pierces the sky above Toronto, a symbol of the city's own reach for the sky.

First Nations People, who inhabited the northern shore of Lake Ontario before the arrival of Europeans, called it Toronto. It meant "meeting place," or "gathering place," because people of different tribes met there. Today, about 80 different ethnic and nationality groups live in this city of 4.4 million residents.

Toronto young people enjoying a snowy day

Ask Torontonians about their city and they will immediately tell you about its diversity. People from places as far away as Korea and Zimbabwe blend with the original British flavor of the city without losing their own identities and customs. Different languages, different faces, different foods, and different beliefs are all part of Toronto's unique personality.

In 1981, 38 percent of the city's population was foreign-born, and a 1989 United Nations survey named Toronto the world's most ethnically cosmopolitan city. It is still a meeting place. The people of the First Nations certainly chose a good name.

The diverse inhabitants of Toronto blend with the flavor of the city without losing their own identities and customs.

One of the first things a visitor to Toronto notices is its many distinct neighborhoods. These seem like a lot of small towns pasted together into a collage. Some of these neighborhoods are made up of people from the same country or ethnic group, while others seem to reflect a lifestyle rather than any particular nationality. These neighborhoods change as one group moves on and another takes its place.

A CITY OF NEIGHBORHOODS

Kensington is the half-hippie, half-immigrant heart of downtown Toronto—lively, noisy, and colorful. Its narrow streets are lined with Victorian houses that have been turned into shops. People of different nationalities mingle there, their voices blending into a lively hubbub. In the 1920s, this was the Jewish market. Today, only one Jewish market remains, Mandell's Dairy, but the streets are still alive with market stalls. A visit to Kensington is like a trip around the world, with shops and shoppers of many different nationalities right next to one another.

Above: "Hippie sunglasses"
Right: Colorful counterculture used-clothing shops crowd a corner of Kensington Market.

Above: A Chinese merchant on Dundas Street, Chinatown
Right: A Chinese cheongsam, a dress with a slit skirt and a mandarin collar

Asians make up the largest percentage of Toronto's immigrant groups, with Chinese the most common. Chinatown, where many Chinese and others of Asian origin have gathered, is thought to be the largest Chinese neighborhood in North America. It is liveliest on Sundays, when Dundas Street is bustling with market stalls selling everything from lotus flowers to wonton skins. A fortune-cookie factory there makes more than 10,000 cookies each day!

Queen West is the Bohemian neighborhood, a mix of restaurants, outdoor cafes, and funky boutiques where trendy fashions mix with New Age. It is one of the most popular shopping districts for young Torontonians, and a center for the latest music. Here also is the City TV building, a television studio with many outdoor events.

Yorkville is an elegant neighborhood of stylish boutiques, designer clothing stores, art galleries, and restaurants, many tucked into little courtyards connected by narrow alleys. Cumberland Park, at its heart, combines gardens, groves of trees, walkways, even a tiny marsh and a large piece of rock from the Canadian Shield, in a space that was once a parking lot.

Little Italy was once home to newly arrived Italian families, but as the Italians have moved northward into other neighborhoods, Portuguese people have moved into their old houses. But it is still the "hometown" of the Italian families who used to live there, its streets lined with trattorias, cafes, and Italian markets. Toronto's Italian population is the largest of any city outside of Italy.

In East Toronto is Greektown, also called the Danforth, filled with restaurants selling authentic Greek foods. In the Indian Bazaar neighborhood, many women wear bright silk saris, the traditional women's dress of India. These are sold in the neighhborhood's shops.

The Indian Bazaar is one of Toronto's many ethnic neighborhoods.

West Toronto's other ethnic neighborhoods include Corso Italia—a posh Italian section—Little Poland, Portugal Village, and Koreatown. All of these neighborhoods are filled with shops and restaurants where people from those countries find their favorite foods.

Perhaps Toronto's most relaxed neighborhood is The Beaches. Its shops, boardwalk, and beach on Lake Ontario are crowded in the summer. The lifestyle of the many students and professors who live in the wooden cottages is casual.

Left: A sidewalk scene in The Beaches, a popular lakefront neighborhood Right and below: Seashells

A CHANGING SKYLINE

The top of the dramatic CN Tower is often lost in the clouds, but when it is visible, it seems to dwarf the rest of Toronto's skyline. Although the First Canadian Place and Scotia Plaza buildings, each about half the height of the CN Tower, seem small by comparison to the CN Tower, they make Toronto's first "skyscrapers" look small. Until the 1960s and 1970s, when the first of the modern skyscrapers was built, Toronto's profile was dominated by the 26-story Royal York Hotel, built in 1929 and by two 34-story buildings built the following year.

Toronto's stunning new skyscrapers are concentrated in the downtown Financial District. Perhaps the most elegant of all the new buildings is Toronto's City Hall, whose curved glass towers wrap around a circular green park. The windows of nearby Royal Bank gleam with glass that is colored by 15,500 pounds (7,030 kilograms) of real gold.

These sleek walls of glass and steel contrast sharply with the ornate old buildings almost at their feet. Old Toronto, the streets where commerce thrived in the glory days of the late 1800s, begins at

Swans on Lake Ontario have a perfect view of Toronto's spectacular city skyline.

Toronto Street, where the monumental Bank of Canada Building is a good introduction to the grand architecture of those times.

Narrow Colburne Street is lined with low buildings decorated with stonework in contrasting colors. The most unique structure in this neighbor-hood is the Flatiron (Gooderham) Building on Front Street. The plain back of this building, originally covered by neighboring buildings, is painted with a clever mural that appears to be windows.

A row of restored Victorian buildings along the south side of Front

Street were once shops with warehouses above them. These ornate buildings are not all that's left of Old Toronto. You can see how the workers lived on Berkeley Street, where a row of tiny workers' houses still stands. The Enoch Turner Schoolhouse (now a museum) is Toronto's oldest, built for the children of those immigrants. Nearby, is the Old Post Office Museum, where visitors can write a letter with a quill pen, close it with old-fashioned sealing wax, and have it postmarked by hand.

The wedge-shaped Flatiron Building (left) was built in 1892. Artist Derek Besant painted a mural depicting windows on the west wall of the building in 1980 (above).

CITY ON A LAKE

Like nearly all great cities, Toronto stands on a body of water that gives it access to the great sea-lanes of the world. Once the hub of Toronto's commerce, the harbor declined in importance and by the 1960s was a run-down area of ugly old warehouses. In 1972, the shore was transformed into Toronto's newest neighborhood, Harbourfront. Now, the shore is an active cultural center, with homes and apartments, an antiques market, a walking trail, and specialty shops.

Although big, luxurious cruise ships no longer dock there regularly, the harbor is still a busy place. A sailing center rents boats and teaches sailing; fishing boats take people onto the lake for salmon; the Metro Police Marine Unit moors rescue and patrol craft there; and ferries and harbor cruises run from the quays.

The ferry takes passengers to Toronto Islands. No cars can go to the islands, and people like to go there to walk and to look at the beautiful gardens. These surround its summer cottages, which were built in the 1920s. Walking and in-line skating paths, parks for picnicking, beaches for swimming, and paddleboats make this a popular place to escape the city on weekends.

The Greater Toronto Area (GTA) adds four more regions to the city itself, making it Canada's largest city and its cultural and economic capital. Each of these regions has its own personality and attractions. On the west, Halton has the beautiful Royal Botanic Gardens and Bruce Trail, a scenic hiking path along the Niagara Escarpment, which reaches an altitude of 1,775 feet (541 meters). Nearby Peel is known for the Living Arts Centre in the town of Mississauga and for the giant Dixie Outlet Mall.

York, to the north, is home to one of the country's finest museums of Canadian artists, the McMichael Collection, and the cottages that surround Lake Simcoe. East of the city, Durham has the Parkwood Estate, with 55 rooms and beautiful gardens.

A young Toronto girl enjoying a summer day

Ferryboats like the one on the left take passengers to the Toronto Islands (above), where the sparkling white geodesic dome called Cinesphere dominates the skyline.

Lake Ontario

Lake Ontario, 193 by 53 miles (311 by 85 kilometers), is the smallest of the chain of five Great Lakes. Except for Lake Michigan, Canada shares these lakes with the United States. Shipping from Lake Ontario can reach the Atlantic Ocean via the St. Lawrence River, which flows from the eastern end of the lake, through Quebec, and into the Gulf of St. Lawrence.

STREETWISE

Toronto's street signs are in different colors, not just to be pretty, but to show people which way they are going. All signs for east-west streets are yellow, to represent the path of the sun. Those marking north-south streets are blue since they all lead to the shore of Lake Ontario.

Running almost due north from the lakefront is Yonge Street, the longest street in the world. It is 1,190 miles (1,915 km) long and winds past Lake Superior all the way to Rainy River in northern Ontario without ever changing its name.

Underneath the skyscrapers of the Financial District is an underground city of 6 miles (10 km) of connecting streets and passageways. More than 1,200 stores and businesses are connected so even in cold, winter weather people can shop and walk from building to building. Shoppers follow signs that say "PATH" to find the underground streets.

Toronto's transit system of nearly 2,500 miles (4,023 km) includes streetcar and bus lines, plus Canada's first subway-system routes. Instead of replacing streetcars, as many cities did, Toronto kept and modernized its street-track system, which is now the largest in the world. Whenever they can, Toronto residents use their public-transit system instead of driving cars on city streets. Twenty-two percent of people who work in the city ride public transport to work, the highest rate of any Canadian city.

Toronto street signs

Friends

LAKE

Toronto had only twelve houses when it was named the capital of Ontario in 1792, only five years after British settlers had bought the 250,000 acres (101,000 hectares) from the chiefs of the Mississauge. From this slow start, Toronto seemed to leap forward in the early 1800s and has not stopped growing since. The place the First Nations People called Toronto looks a lot different today than it did when its shores were covered in forests.

FIRST ARRIVALS

Aboriginal people came to the western end of Lake Ontario about 1000 B.C. They lived by hunting, fishing, and growing vegetable crops, particularly corn. Before the Europeans came, the Seneca and later the Mississauge tribes lived in a village they called Teiaiagon, on the northern shore. This spot, where the Humber River enters the lake, is a short distance west of today's downtown.

Those people were part of the larger language group called the Iroquois League, a group of five First Nations People who inhabited large areas of land in what is now northern New York and Ontario.

The story of European exploration and settlement begins many miles east of Toronto, with French explorer Jacques Cartier, who sailed to the New World in 1536. He was stopped abruptly on his way west by the rapids of the St. Lawrence River at Montreal. But his stories made others dream of discovering a waterway to Asia, and his trip marked the beginning of the French colony of New France. In 1603, another French explorer, Samuel de Champlain, who later founded the city of Quebec, was also stopped by the rapids.

Samuel de Champlain

Trapping for beaver

Bartering for Christmas dinner at a Hudson's Bay Company trading post

The French exchanged beads, axes, and other European goods for the tanned skins of beaver, used to make hats, which had become popular among fashionable Europeans. As the demand for beaver skins grew, trappers went farther and farther into the wilderness. They traveled by canoe, which could be carried around rapids.

One of these trappers, Étienne Brulé, was sent by Champlain in 1615 to try to find a water route across the continent. When he reached Lake Ontario, he found the village of Teiaiagon. While Brulé did not begin a city, many more people from the French colony followed him to the area in search of beaver and game.

Settlers on the north shore of the lake began calling the settlement *Toronto*, meaning "meeting place," as the Iroquois did.

The French were not alone in their search for beaver pelts, however. The British tried to take over the fur trade, and formed the Hudson's Bay Company to trade with the First Nations People. To help maintain their control in the face of the better organized British trading company, the French built a small trading post in 1720, near the village of Teiaiagon.

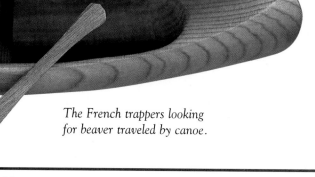

The French trappers looking for beaver traveled by canoe.

WAR IN EUROPE AND THE COLONIES

Early in the 1700s, France and England were at war in Europe, and their war spread to the New World colonies as the French and Indian Wars. The French built a fortification called Fort Rouillé in 1750 to protect the trading post at Teiaiagon from the British, and both the French and the British conducted raids along their North American borders.

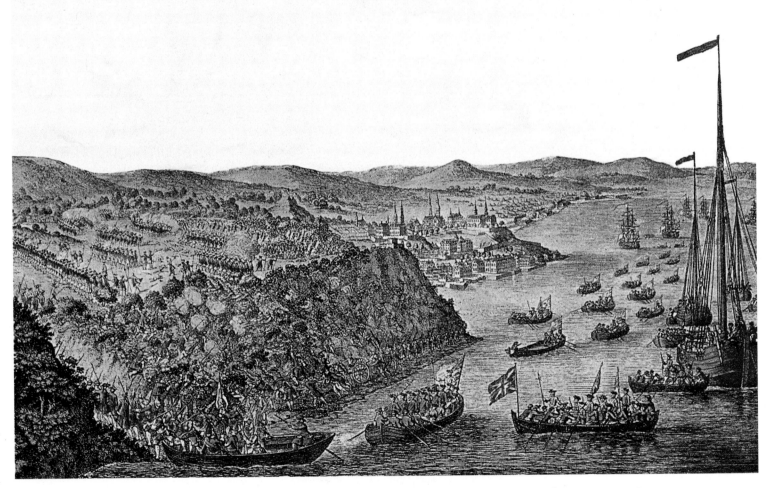

The French and Indian War ended in Canada in 1759, when the British defeated the French army at Quebec City.

A 1755 battle scene during the French and Indian War

The war in Canada ended when the British defeated the French army in 1759 at Quebec City. With their victory, the British destroyed the French forts at Toronto, but the trading post continued to do business with the First Nations People.

Only sixteen years later, the American Revolutionary War began. Britain would lose its thirteen southern colonies in that war, leaving them only the northern territory that had been New France. But that same war brought new settlers north to Toronto. About 40,000 British colonists who stayed loyal to Britain left the new United States and went into the Great Lakes area.

British soldiers ready for battle on the morning of the final confrontation of the French and Indian War in Canada

A TOWN AT LAST

While many people lived around the trading post, it wasn't until 1787 that the governor-in-chief of British North America, Guy Carleton, Baron Dorchester, made a contract to buy a large tract of land. He paid three chiefs of the Mississauge tribe £1,700 and a supply of axes, cloth, and food for the 250,000 acres (101,172 hectares) where the city now stands.

The new settlement at Toronto had a lot going for it. It had access to the sea. A good harbor was protected from Great Lakes gales by islands and a peninsula. The settlement was also an established trading post, with a record of peace with the neighboring First Nations People. The lake shaped Ontario's early growth. Busy harbors at each river's mouth enabled ships to supply the traders and settlers and move their furs and farm produce to markets.

A street was built along the waterfront, and by 1790, another was laid out to the north, opening up the backcountry. Called Yonge Street, it was later extended 1,190 miles (1,915 km) into northern Ontario, making it the longest street in the world.

Only two years later, the village of only twelve houses was selected to be the capital of Ontario by Lieutenant Governor John Simcoe. He laid out streets in a grid pattern and renamed the town York in honor of the king's son, the Duke of York. Simcoe hoped this would get Toronto favorable attention from the king. His legislature, called the Assembly, passed a law prohibiting slavery in Ontario, years before Britain outlawed it.

Sir Guy Carleton, governor-in-chief of British North America from 1786 to 1791

When Britain and the United States went to war in 1812, Toronto was a town of 700 people. It was captured twice by the Americans and was destroyed in 1813. But the town was rebuilt and prospered. The end of the War of 1812, while it did not end military blustering on both sides of the border for many years, did end actual fighting.

Commercial and social contact across the borders grew.

Costumed musicians at Fort York

Seeing Early Toronto Firsthand

Fort York re-creates life in a British garrison during the War of 1812 when the city was under attack by American troops. Military demonstrations, music, cooking demonstrations, and a theater in the blockhouse help show how soldiers and their families lived. At Campbell House, costumed guides take visitors through a mansion built ten years later, showing the life of a wealthy family in more peaceful times.

GROWTH AND GOVERNMENT REFORM

Population swelled when people left England after the European wars with Napoleon. York became a city in 1834 and took back its old name of Toronto. The thriving city no longer needed to keep the king happy. Its population had risen from 720 in 1816 to 9,252 in 1834.

In 1827, King's College was chartered. It opened to students in 1843 and later became the University of Toronto. About this time, the city became active in the reform movements that swept Canada from the 1830s. Up to that time, the British government in London decided who would govern Canada. Now Canada had become more self-sufficient, and Canadians wanted to govern themselves.

In Toronto, W. W. Baldwin and Robert Baldwin, who had come to the city from Ireland, began to urge that Canada be allowed to have a Cabinet system of government. The locally elected assembly should appoint the lieutenant governor and executive council, they argued. This would give the assembly control of the executive branch and limit the power of the British-appointed governor. Other political leaders favored a system of divided powers like that in the neighboring United States. William Lyon Mackenzie, Toronto's first mayor, was so active in his reform movement that he almost started a revolution. He was forced to leave Toronto and Canada for many years.

The town of York (originally called Toronto) as it looked in 1803

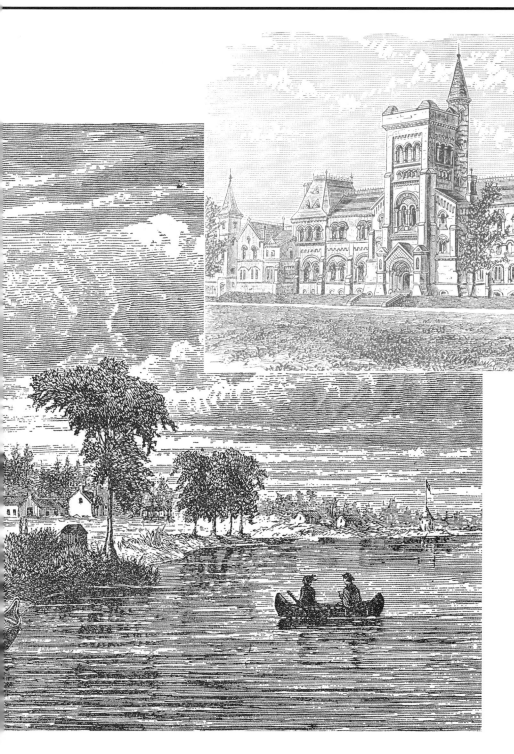

King's College (above and below), now called the University of Toronto, opened to students in 1843.

BOOMTOWN

The city continued to grow with each new wave of immigration. By the 1830s, the first Jewish people came, and in 1847, they were joined by 40,000 Irish fleeing starvation from the potato famine.

In the mid 1800s, businessmen saw the railroads as a way to make money. Political leaders saw them as a way to bring the separated parts of the big country together. The Grand Trunk and Great Western Railway reached the city in the 1850s, about the same time that telegraph, roads, canals, and shipping increased contact with the rest of Canada and the world.

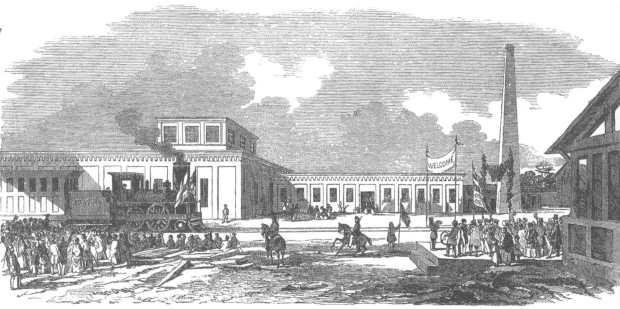

The Grand Trunk and Great Western Railway reached Toronto in 1854.

Even a fire in 1849 that destroyed 15 acres (6 ha) of downtown Toronto, including St. James Cathedral, the St. Lawrence Market, stores, and offices, was only a temporary setback to the growing city. In 1854, a treaty with the United States led to free trade across the border for many types of goods. Huge areas of forest-land north of the city were cut into lumber for the Canadian and United States markets. Toronto was poised for success.

Left: Toronto as it looked in 1858

30

By 1861, more than 45,000 people lived in the city. In the 1880s, persecution of Jews in eastern Europe and Russia sent another large group to Toronto. Settlers poured into the country and the city from all over eastern and central Europe over the next 20 years. Economic hard times and wars encouraged people to take advantage of Canadian government offers of free or inexpensive passage for immigrants. At the turn of the century, the population reached 208,000, a gain of more than 207,000 people in only 85 years.

Above: An early lithograph of King Street, Toronto, by Nathaniel Currier

THE GLORY DAYS

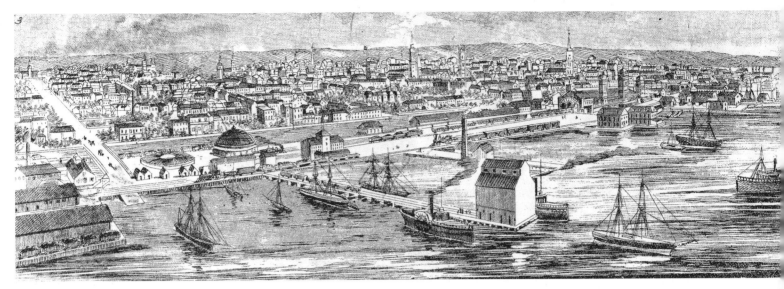

Toronto in 1881

Lieutenant Governor Simcoe had chosen a good site for his town. It had a wonderful harbor to bring in goods and to ship its products. Productive farmland around it could supply much of the city's food, with extra to sell. The forests in the empty lands to the north provided huge amounts of lumber for shipment to growing markets in eastern Canada and the United States. The railroad continued to help Toronto grow as the city became the rail terminal for the expanding West, tying all Canada together.

Toronto's position as a rail center, the development of the port of Toronto, and final settlement of border disputes with the United States made the future of the city secure. It became a hub of shipping from the Canadian and American West through the Great Lakes and the St. Lawrence River Valley. Great canals and locks were built to allow big ships to carry huge cargoes of grain from the prairies and minerals from the mines of the West. Farming displaced logging, and industry developed to take advantage of the city's location.

When the Canadian Confederation was formed in 1867, Toronto became the capital of the new province of Ontario. Toronto's new importance and wealth was reflected in the buildings that rose beside the lake. The Old City Hall, the Provincial Assembly Building, and rows of ornately decorated business blocks grew in the downtown area. Street after street of fine homes spread outward from the center, homes for those who profited from Toronto's growing prosperity. Living standards rose for workers, too, as running water, electricity, and central heating reached more and more homes.

*Toronto's legislative building
in Queen's Park*

Only the Great Depression, which quickly spread into Canada from the United States in the 1930s, slowed down the constant hum of Toronto's machinery. Unemployment rose to 30 percent as companies cut back production or shut down altogether.

World War II restored prosperity, as factories and farms cranked up production to supply the armies of the British Commonwealth. Again, widespread destruction in Europe brought yet another influx of immigrants after the war ended in 1945.

*Queen Elizabeth and King George VI visiting
wounded World War II veterans at Christie
Hospital*

THE CHANGING FACES OF TORONTO

The two World Wars each sent new waves of immigrants to Toronto in the 1920s, 1930s, and 1940s. In the 1970s and 1980s, people fleeing the unrest of war, economic hard times, and political instability in Asia, South America, and the Middle East poured into the city, changing its character yet again.

Tens of thousands of immigrants from all over Asia fled to Canada and especially to Toronto. Chinese, Koreans, Vietnamese, Laotians, and Cambodians all brought their influences, taking their places next to the British, French, Italian, Polish, and other peoples who came before them.

South Americans, West Indians, and Muslims from the Middle East also enriched the cultural diversity of the city. About one-fourth of all immigrants who have come to Canada since the 1950s and 1960s have settled in Toronto. The joining of all of these cultures in the city has made it a bright, bubbling, and fascinating montage of the world.

The 1960s and 1970s saw dramatic changes in Toronto's skyline, as the sleek, modern skyscrapers of the Financial District rose above the city. Unlike many other cities, Toronto did not build on its original center, east of Yonge Street. Instead, it moved slowly westward, so many buildings from the glory days were not torn down to make way for today's skyscrapers. Toronto continues to be a city of cutting-edge architecture, using the latest new designs for its buildings, while preserving the best of its old ones.

The joining of many cultures has made Toronto a fascinating montage of the world.

*Toronto teens rehearsing
a script for a play*

*During the 1960s and
1970s, the sleek,
modern skyscrapers of
the Financial District
rose above the city.*

TORONTO

Toronto has become one of Canada's major destinations for tourists, who remark at the city's cleanliness, low crime rate, and ethnic diversity. Torontonians enjoy their city just as much as the many tourists who visit it. Toronto is the world's greenest city, with at least ten trees for every person living there. Whether they are in-line skating along the lakefront path or taking a short-cut through a park to their office in a skyscraper, Torontonians enjoy the diversity of their city on the lake.

TORONTO AT WORK . . .

Toronto is the finance and banking capital of Canada. Much of the financing for industries all over Canada begins in the skyscrapers on Bay Street, where 90 percent of the country's chartered-bank assets are located. The Stock Exchange, at First Canadian Place, is the country's largest, with 80 percent of Canada's trading and 1,300 companies listed.

Stock and bond trading was formalized in the city as early as 1852, when the Toronto Stock Exchange was created. A frieze decorating the old Stock Exchange on Bay Street shows Canada's diverse manufacturing, in a design of workers with cogs, girders, tools, and automobiles.

Automobiles are manufactured in the suburbs of Oakville, Brampton, and Oshawa, and about 90 percent of these are exported to the United States. Redpath Sugar, which moved to Toronto when the St. Lawrence Seaway made it easier to ship its product all over the world, makes 1,000 tons (900 metric tons) of sugar each day. Its tall silos near Queen's Quay are part of Toronto's skyline.

Above: A mural on the Redpath Sugar silo
Right: The Toronto Stock Exchange information center

This view of downtown Toronto includes the modern Roy Thomson Hall (left front)

Toronto is also the communications capital, with CBC (Canadian Broadcasting Corporation) and CTV networks both headquartered there. In 1952, CBC pioneered in television broadcasting in Canada. Most English-language program production still centers in Toronto. Northern Telecom, the second largest telecommunications company in North America, has its headquarters in suburban Toronto. A center for printing and publishing, the city is home to most of Canada's major magazines, such as *McLean's*. The *Toronto Globe and Mail* is a nationally circulated newspaper.

AND AT PLAY

A chandelier weighing 1,300 pounds (590 kg) has crashed to the floor more than 4,000 times since 1989, each crash ending act one of *The Phantom of the Opera* at the Pantages Theatre. More than 6 million tickets have been sold, and tapes and CD sales of the Canadian cast reach over 800,000 copies. Agatha Christie's mystery *The Mousetrap* has been playing in Toronto for 22 years, longer than any other North American stage production.

These record-breaking shows are only two of the theater and musical performances Torontonians can choose from each evening. Thirteen major theaters, an opera company, a symphony orchestra, and a ballet company are just the beginning of entertainment possibilities, which also include performances in several concert halls, dinner theaters, cabarets, and clubs.

An entire theater, Toronto Puppet Centre, is reserved for puppet shows for young people. Even the coatracks and water fountains are within reach of young visitors, who sit on the floor to watch performances by more than four dozen professional puppet and marionette companies.

Toronto is a favorite location for filming movies, so it is not unusual to find film crews in the streets or stars having dinner in the city's restaurants. *Good Will Hunting, Map of the World, Moonstruck,* and *Three Men and a Baby* have been shot there recently. The Royal York Hotel is a popular movie set, and "home away from home" to the many stars who come to the city. Bob Hope, Frank Sinatra, Dolly Parton, David Copperfield, and Morgan Fairchild are just a few of the stars who have stayed there. Television's *The X-Files* was filmed in Toronto until 1999.

The Puppet Princess, shown here, might have starred in a Toronto Puppet Centre production.

On Tour

Tours of the Pantages Theatre, originally the largest vaudeville house in the entire British Empire, take visitors through the "marble" lobby (it's actually plaster painted so realistically that people have to touch it to tell the difference) and into the backstage workings. Here they learn about all the special effects that this extra-large stage is famous for.

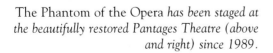

The Phantom of the Opera *has been staged at the beautifully restored Pantages Theatre (above and right) since 1989.*

Children playing in a Henry Moore
sculpture at the Art Gallery of Ontario

A stained-glass maple leaf
suncatcher created by a
talented artist from Canada

A HOME FOR THE ARTS

The Royal Ontario Museum, known to locals as the ROM, is Canada's largest museum. Six million objects fill more than 40 galleries, and 1,200 pieces of Chinese art form one of the finest collections outside of China. The world's best collection of Canadian decorative arts, a gallery devoted to Korean art, masks of the First Nations People, and Egyptian mummy cases highlight its art collections, while other parts of the museum feature gemstones, dinosaurs, and other science exhibits.

The Art Gallery of Ontario has 18,000 paintings, sculptures, and other art that include works by Rembrandt and Picasso, as well as Canadian artists.

The McMichael Canadian Art Gallery, north of the city in Kleinburg, was built to house a major collection of twentieth-century Canadian art. The museum shows the paintings of Canada's impressionist artists, known as the Group of Seven. These seven painters of the early 1900s were also known as the "Fathers of Canadian Impressionism."

Throughout the city are other fine collections: Canadian paintings in a department store, Inuit art at Toronto Dominion Bank, medieval art at the University of Toronto, and more than 70 art galleries.

Right: A sculpture at the Royal Ontario Museum
Below: The Art Gallery of Ontario

HOMETOWN TEAMS

People in Toronto love sports and support their professional teams. In 1989, the city built the state-of-the-art SkyDome in the center of the city. Its roof rolls back in good weather, and people staying in the tall SkyDome Hotel can look right down into it to watch games from their rooms.

The SkyDome is the home stadium for the Blue Jays, Toronto's baseball team. In 1997, their pitcher, Roger Clemens, led the American League with a 21–7 season and 292 strikeouts. The Argonauts are members of the Canadian Football League, and in 1991 and 1996 they won the championship, called the Grey Cup.

Above: The SkyDome

Left: Toronto Blue Jay player Casey Blake

The Maple Leafs, Toronto's hockey team, hold their games in the Air Canada Centre, completed in 1999. The Toronto Raptors, members of the National Basketball Association, also play in the Centre.

Toronto is home to the Hockey Hall of Fame, in an ornate former bank building on Yonge Street. The coveted Stanley Cup, presented to championship teams, is on display there.

It Happened in Toronto

Babe Ruth hit the first home run of his professional career on Hanlan's Point, on the Toronto Islands, on September 5, 1914.

Hockey's coveted Stanley Cup is on display in Toronto's Hockey Hall of Fame.

Everyone loves taking the most exciting ride in Toronto, in a glass elevator whizzing to the top of the CN Tower in less than a minute. From there, you can see for miles in every direction. Only the bravest dare to stand on the glass floor panels that allow you to look straight down at the street, 1,122 feet (342 m) directly underfoot.

A VIEW FROM THE TOP

From the CN Tower you can look down onto the SkyDome and Ontario Place, a cultural and leisure center quickly recognized by the geodesic dome of Cinesphere, which houses the IMAX theater. Children's Village there is a state-of-the-art playground, the first one like it in North America. An outdoor water-play area has rapids and waterfalls to slide down.

The Pier, a waterfront museum, is a good place to find out how Toronto grew from its first settlement of fur traders to one of Canada's greatest ports of the Industrial Revolution. Model ships show craft that plied the lake, from canoes made of birchbark to modern container ships. Craftsmen in the Boat Shop build wooden boats, which visitors can rent to explore the harbor. The famous Canadian warship, the destroyer HMCS *Haida*, is open to visitors in the summer, when it is not being used as a training ship for cadet mariners. A schooner takes passengers for lake rides under billowing canvas sails in the summer.

Inside the St. Lawrence Market building, stalls offer everything from used books to old kitchen utensils.

A view of Ontario Place, a cultural and leisure center spread over three islands in Lake Ontario

The busy St. Lawrence Market, a few blocks away on Front Street, is made up of parts of Toronto's old City Hall. Saturdays are busiest here, when farmers from the rich lands around Toronto gather on the streets outside to sell vegetables, flowers, and plants. Inside the brick building are flea-market stalls selling everything from used books to old kitchen utensils.

Toronto's Metro Zoo brings almost a million people a year to its 710-acre (287-ha) grounds, where 459 species of creatures live. This is Canada's largest zoo, and the third largest in North America. Among its most popular residents are rare Komodo dragons, which are giant lizards.

A tiger at the Metro Zoo

THREE TORONTO SURPRISES

Shoes may seem like an unlikely subject for a museum, but the Bata Shoe Museum is one of the city's liveliest places to visit. Shoes tell us a lot about how people live and what they do, and in the displays are spiked clogs for crushing chestnuts, tiny shoes for the bound feet of Chinese women, *Apollo* space boots, and Egyptian sandals more than 4,000 years old. Some famous shoes include those worn by Princess Diana, Elvis Presley, and John Lennon. Visitors learn some interesting facts, including the origin of the word "sabotage": workers during the French Revolution shut down factories by throwing their *sabots* (the French word for "shoes") into the machines.

A view of the Bata Shoe Museum

Visitors enjoy touring Casa Loma, an extravagant castle built by railway baron Sir Henry Pellatt.

Casa Loma is an extravagant castle built by railway baron Sir Henry Pellatt. He borrowed ideas from his favorite castles in Europe to build his estate with secret passages, tunnels, gargoyles, towers, gardens, and stables that are more luxurious than many houses. During World War II, those stables hid the production site for the top-secret sonar device called ASDIC after its original workshop in London was bombed.

Amateur sleuths love to visit the Metropolitan Police Museum, where interactive displays and games show how police investigate crimes. Visitors try their hands at solving crimes, learn to tell real from counterfeit money, and see a police station from the year 1929.

People of all ages, especially young people, enjoy visiting the Metropolitan Police Museum, which has interactive displays and games.

FESTIVALS AND CELEBRATIONS

Multicultural is the key word to describe Toronto's busy calendar of holidays and festivals. Perhaps the most colorful is the International Dragon Boat Festival in June, when more than 160 teams race colorful 38-foot (12-meter) dragon boats off Toronto's islands. Although this is an important Chinese cultural event, people from many other cultures perform and sell their ethnic foods.

Caribana, in July, fills the city with West Indian sounds and a colorful all-day parade of steel bands and dancers in elaborate costumes. Metro International Caravan, also in July, showcases foods, crafts, music, dance, and other activities at 40 pavilions representing different cultures.

A costumed participant in Caribana, a colorful celebration put on by Toronto's West Indian communities

Everyone, no matter what their own religious or ethnic background, loves to see Toronto dressed for Christmas. The Eaton Centre, a downtown shopping complex, is filled with huge decorations. Many stores display decorated windows and animated Christmas scenes, but none can compare to the lavish displays at the Hudson's Bay Company.

Thousands and thousands of tiny colored lights decorate trees along Queen Street, and brightly dressed skaters swirl around the ice rink at City Hall. The season begins with the Santa Claus Parade in late November, watched on television by millions of people around the world.

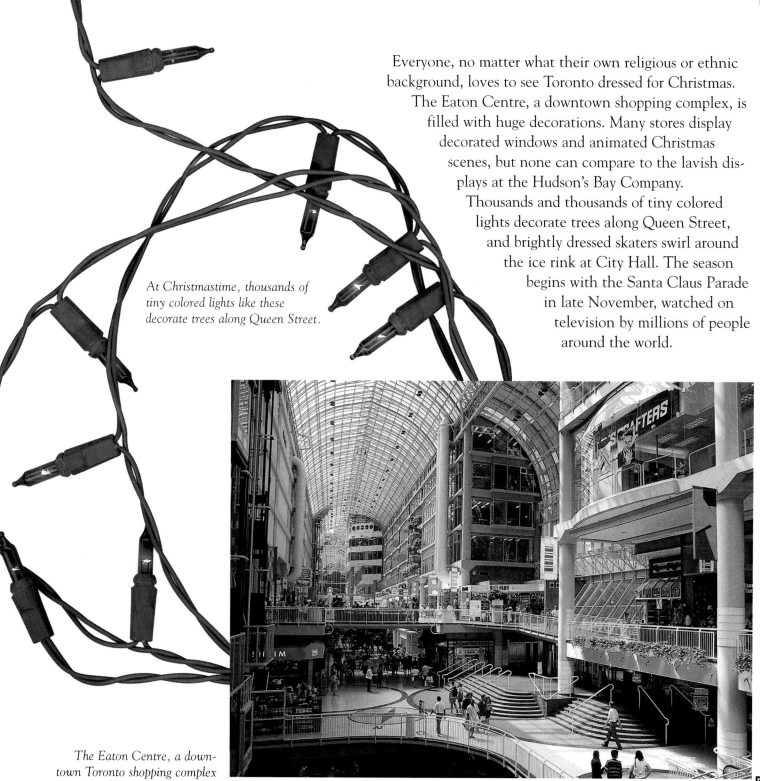

At Christmastime, thousands of tiny colored lights like these decorate trees along Queen Street.

The Eaton Centre, a downtown Toronto shopping complex

LIVING IN TORONTO

Although Toronto's inner city has some poor neighborhoods, there are no ghettos. The crime rate is low and a growing number of people are choosing to live in the city's core. A survey taken in 1993 rated it as one of the four most livable cities in North America.

Many people of different income levels live in the city, especially in the new Harbourfront area. Rent at some of the apartments there is based on income, or they are reserved for elderly people so those without a lot of money can live there. Other buildings have very expensive luxury apartments and condominiums. Residential neighborhoods change with the years, as shown by the area known as Cabbagetown. Once described as a slum, the area got its name from the smell of cabbage cooking in the kitchens of the Irish immigrants who lived there.

Rent at some Harbourfront apartments (above) is based on income or reserved for elderly people.

Left: A smiling Iranian resident of Toronto

*Left: An elegrant
home in Rosedale,
one of Toronto's
wealthiest suburbs*

*Below: A young Toronto
girl enjoying a sunny day*

Recently, however, its small homes have been restored
and the area has become quite fashionable.

Around Toronto are suburbs filled with residential
streets, most of which are lined with one-family houses. Two of the wealthiest neighborhoods in the city are
Rosedale, set in a ravine, and Forest Hill, a tree-filled
area of elegant homes.

FAMOUS LANDMARKS

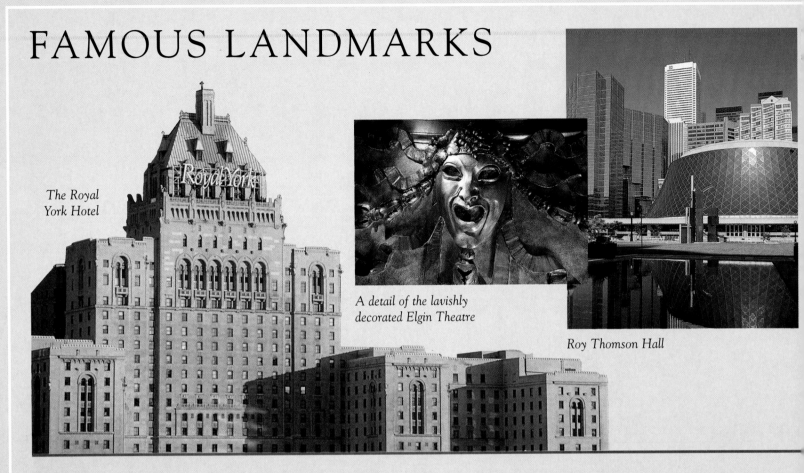

The Royal York Hotel

A detail of the lavishly decorated Elgin Theatre

Roy Thomson Hall

CN Tower
At 1,815 feet (553 m) tall, the CN Tower is the tallest self-supporting structure in the world, almost twice as tall as the Eiffel Tower in Paris and nearly 500 feet (152 m) taller than the World Trade Center in New York City. Views reach up to 100 miles (161 km) from the observation deck at the top.

SkyDome
Right under the CN Tower, this stadium seats 50,516 spectators and has a roll-back roof that opens to the sky in 20 minutes, but can withstand snowdrifts of 11.5 feet (3.5 m). It has artificial turf, contains twice as much concrete as the CN Tower, and the pitcher's mound disappears when the diamond becomes a football field.

Roy Thomson Hall
A circular building of square and triangle-shaped glass panels, Roy Thomson Hall is Toronto's main concert hall, with a wraparound lobby surrounding the hall itself. The Toronto Symphony plays there.

Elgin and Wintergarden Theatres
The last double-decker theater complex still operating in the world, the downstairs Elgin is lavishly decorated, while the upstairs Wintergarden has tree-trunk columns and a ceiling of leaves.

Fort York
Toronto's earliest days are re-created in this fort where soldiers defended their settlement from American troops during the War of 1812. Costumed guides demonstrate the cooking, music, and military life of the period.

Bay Street
Art Deco skyscrapers built in the 1920s and 1930s, the first tall buildings in Toronto, form a canyon along the street. The Concourse Building at the corner of Adelaide Street and the Sterling Tower at the corner of Richmond are two of the most beautiful.

University of Toronto
Right in the middle of the city, the university campus looks like an English college and is often used in filming movies set in England. Its stone buildings combine medieval gargoyles, carved columns, arches, and cloisters.

Pantages Theatre
Once the British Empire's largest vaudeville theater, this building is where The Phantom of the Opera has played since 1989.

Harbourfront

Grimacing faces over the front entrance of Old City Hall

The top of the CN Tower

Union Station
Designed, it is said, after Roman baths, the soaring interior of the station has names of Canadian cities spelled in giant letters around the top.

Royal Ontario Museum
Canada's largest museum has medieval armor, dinosaurs, a Chinese tomb, diamonds, a bat cave, and a special section just for children, which children helped design.

Old City Hall
The architect of this building on Queen Street was so annoyed when the city councilors refused to put his name on the corner-stone, that he carved their grimacing faces over the front entrance. They look like gargoyles, but everyone could recognize the councilors.

Bata Shoe Museum
More than 10,000 shoes from all times and places, worn by famous and unknown people, are collected in a building designed to resemble a shoe box.

Hudson's Bay Outfitters
The Hudson's Bay Company, older than Canada itself, is a unique, newly designed store that has everything for a Canadian outdoor vacation, sold in a setting complete with an indoor waterfall and a 1930s bush plane.

The Royal York Hotel
Once the largest and tallest building in the British Empire, the Royal York was built in 1929 by the Canadian Pacific Railroad, close to Union Station, as the flagship of its chain of grand hotels for its passengers.

Eaton Centre
This giant 15-acre (6-ha) indoor shopping complex built around a plant-filled atrium, has more than 300 shops, restaurants, and cafes.

Harbourfront
Once a rundown area of old warehouses facing the docks, the waterfront is now filled with modern apartment buildings, shops, museums, and places for Torontonians to spend their leisure time. Harbourfront Centre is a year-round setting for arts, performances, and recreation.

High Park
The city's largest park lies to the west, a vast area with walking and bicycle trails, tennis courts, a swimming beach, a skating pond, wildflowers, and even an enclosure of buffalo, llamas, and sheep. Shakespeare's plays are performed in High Park in the summer.

FAST FACTS

POPULATION (1996):

City: 2,400,000

Metropolitan Area: 4,444,700

AREA 2,156 square miles
(5,584 sq km)

CLIMATE Toronto is farther south than most Canadian cities so its climate is milder than any except those on the Pacific Coast. January is the coldest month, with an average daytime temperature of 27.5 degrees Fahrenheit (−2.5° Celsius) and nighttime temperature of 52 degrees Fahrenheit (11.1° Celsius). July, the warmest month, averages a high of 80 degrees Fahrenheit (27° Celsius) and a low of 57.5 degrees Fahrenheit (14.2° Celsius). Included in the city's 32 inches (81 centimeters) of annual precipitation is 5.5 inches (14 cm) of snow. About 139 days a year have wet weather.

INDUSTRY Toronto is Canada's finance and banking capital, with 90 percent of its bank assets and the largest Stock Exchange, where 80 percent of Canada's stock is traded. Also the communications capital, Toronto is home to the Canadian Broadcasting Corporation, which produces most of its English-language programs there, and to Northern Telecom, North America's second largest telecommunications company. Canada's printing and publishing are also centered in Toronto. Automobiles are manufactured in the suburbs, most for export to the United States. Redpath Sugar, sold all over the world, makes 1,000 tons (900 metric tons) of sugar in Toronto each day.

CHRONOLOGY

1000 B.C.
Human beings arrive on the northern shore of Lake Ontario.

A.D. 1720
A small fur-trading post is built by the French in New France.

1750
French traders build the first forts.

1759
The English destroy French forts, but the trading post remains.

1775–1778
British subjects loyal to the king leave the lower thirteen colonies and settle in Toronto.

1787
Guy Carleton buys land for a town from the First Nations People.

1790
Yonge Street is laid out from the lake into the northern backcountry.

1792
Toronto (then called York) is named the capital of Ontario Territory.

1813
American forces capture and destroy the town during the War of 1812.

1834
York becomes a city and takes back the name of Toronto.

1850s
The Grand Trunk and Great Western Railways reach Toronto.

1867
Toronto becomes the capital of the new Province of Ontario.

1879
Standard Time is invented by Sir Stanford Fleming at the University of Toronto.

Swan boat rides on Centre Island

1914–1918
World War I sends new waves of European immigrants to Toronto.

1930s
The Great Depression hits Toronto, causing unemployment of 30 percent of the workforce.

1939–1945
World War II causes another wave of immigration.

1954
The Municipality of Metropolitan Toronto is formed, and the subway opens.

1960–1975
Unrest in Southeast Asia, South America, and the Middle East brings more immigrants.

1970s
English-speaking people leaving Montreal settle in Toronto.

1972
David Crombie is elected mayor and begins program of reforms.

1990
Underground passageways connecting downtown buildings are completed.

TORONTO

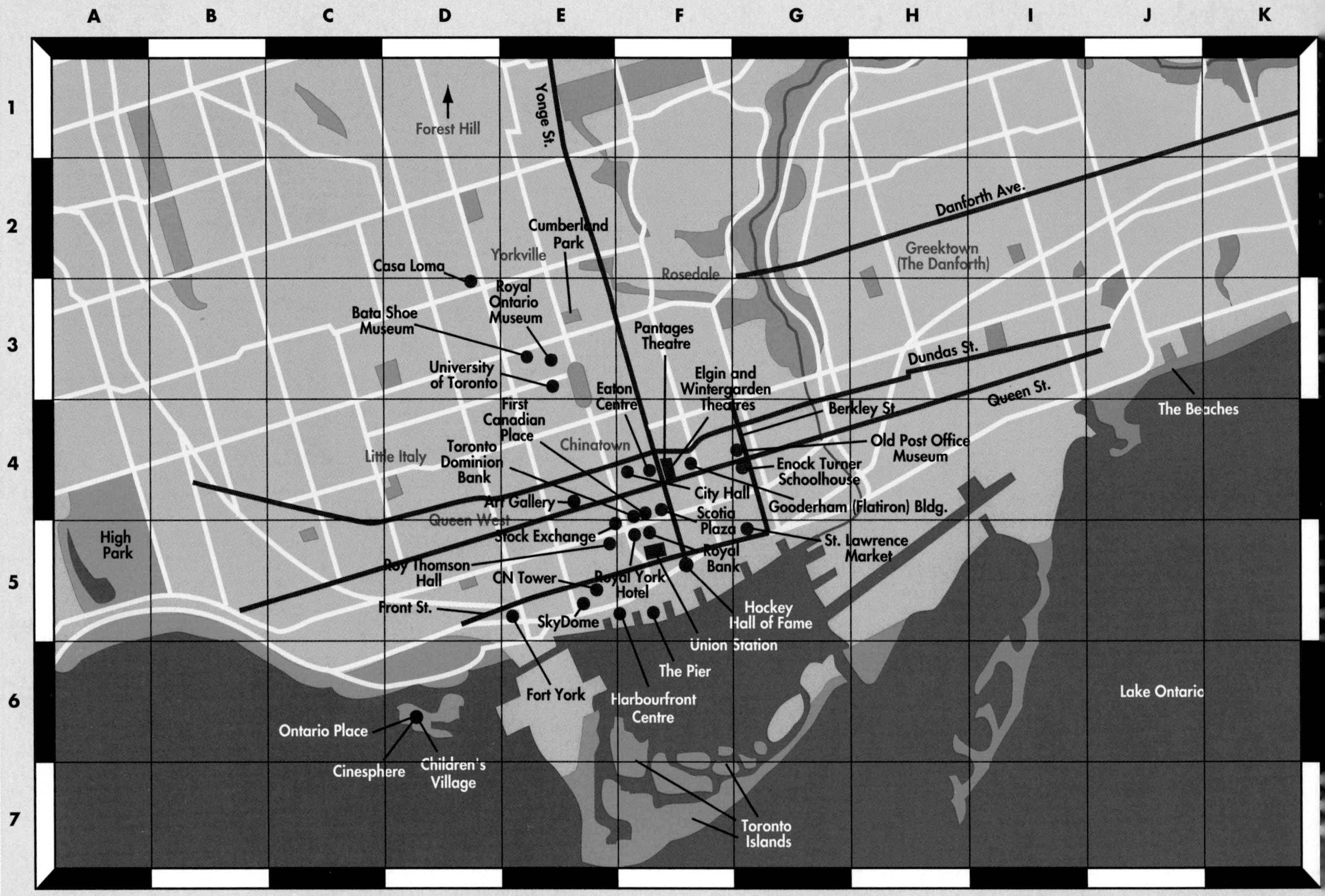

Map labels (on map):

A B C D E F G H I J K (columns)
1–7 (rows)

Forest Hill · Yonge St. · Danforth Ave. · Cumberland Park · Yorkville · Rosedale · Greektown (The Danforth) · Casa Loma · Royal Ontario Museum · Bata Shoe Museum · Pantages Theatre · Dundas St. · University of Toronto · Elgin and Wintergarden Theatres · Eaton Centre · Berkley St · Queen St. · First Canadian Place · Chinatown · The Beaches · Little Italy · Toronto Dominion Bank · Old Post Office Museum · Enock Turner Schoolhouse · Art Gallery · Gooderham (Flatiron) Bldg. · City Hall · Scotia Plaza · Stock Exchange · Queen West · High Park · St. Lawrence Market · Roy Thomson Hall · CN Tower · Royal York Hotel · Royal Bank · Front St. · Hockey Hall of Fame · SkyDome · Union Station · The Pier · Fort York · Harbourfront Centre · Lake Ontario · Ontario Place · Cinesphere · Children's Village · Toronto Islands

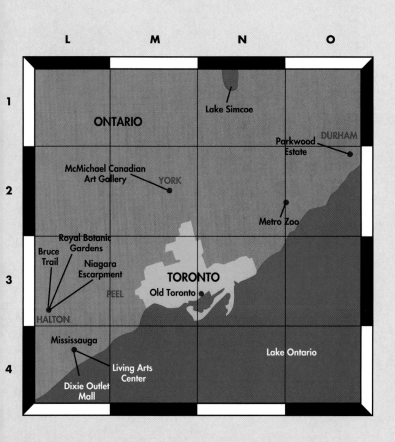

GLOSSARY

Art Deco: A style of architecture and decoration popular in the early twentieth century

British Empire: The nations and territories that once were ruled by Great Britain, including Canada, Australia, New Zealand, India, and much of Africa

Canadian Shield: The rock surface that lies beneath most of Central Canada

dim sum: Steamed Chinese dumplings

First Nations People: Canada's Native Americans

frieze: A band of sculpture that decorates a building

girder: A steel beam used in constructing buildings

quay: Dock or pier where ships moor

schooner: A style of sailing ship, usually with two or three masts

St. Lawrence Seaway: A waterway system of locks to take large ships from the Great Lakes to the Atlantic Ocean

trattoria: A small, informal Italian restaurant

vaudeville: Stage variety shows popular in the 1800s and early 1900s

Victorian: The ornate decorative style of the period when Queen Victoria ruled the British Empire, which included most of the 1800s

TORONTO & SURROUNDINGS

Picture Identifications

Cover: Toronto skyline; a smiling freckled girl
Page 1: Queen Street, Toronto
Pages 4–5: Toronto skyline at sunset, CN Tower on left
Pages 8–9: Colorful murals and zany storefronts in the Queen Street West area of Toronto
Pages 20–21: A French fur trapper meeting members of the First Nations People
Pages 36–37: In-line skaters on the Martin Goodman Trail along the Lake Ontario waterfront
Page 37: A bear tourist magnet
Pages 46-47: The Provincial Parliament building in Queen's Park, Toronto

Photo Credits ©

Chris Snell — Cover (background), 1, 27, 38 (both pictures), 43 (both pictures), 55 (left), 57 (middle)
Photo Edit — Amy C. Etra, cover (foreground); Steve Skjold, 6; Myrleen Ferguson, 7 (bottom), 55 (right); Tony Freeman, 16, 54 (left); David Young-Wolff, 19 (bottom), 34 (top), 51; Michael Newman, 35 (top)
KK&A, Ltd. — 3, 10 (left), 11 (right), 13 (right), 23 (bottom), 37, 40, 42 (bottom), 53 (left), 60, 61
Tom Stack & Associates — Thomas Kitchin, 4-5, 17 (bottom), 18, 34–35, 46–47, 49 (top), 57 (left and right); Matt Bradley, 39
Liaison Agency — 25 (top); Alain Buu, 7 (top); Jed Jacobsohn, 44 (bottom)
Dave G. Houser — 10 (right), 11 (left), 12, 13 (left), 36-37; Jan Butchofsky-Houser, 8–9
New England Stock Photo — Jim Schnabel, 14; John C. Whyte, 15 (right), 49 (bottom)
H. Armstrong Roberts — D. Lada, 15 (left), 29 (bottom)
Peter Mintz — 17 (top), 41 (bottom), 45, 59
Woodfin Camp & Associates — Jim Anderson, 19 (top); Mike Yamashita, 42 (top), 50 (top)
Corbis/Bettmann — 20–21, 26, 29 (top), 31, 32, 33 (both pictures)
Stock Montage, Inc. — 22 (top), 23 (top), 28–29, 30 (both pictures)
North Wind Pictures — 22 (bottom), 24
North Wind Picture Archives — 25 (bottom)
Hill Peppard — 41 (top)
Tony Stone Images, Inc. — John Edwards, 44 (top)
Robert Fried — 48
The Image Finders — Michael Philip Manheim, 50 (bottom)
Tony Sladden — 52
Wolfgang Kaehler — 53 (right), 56 (left and right)
Unicorn Stock Photos L.L.C. — Andre Jenny, 54 (right)
Danita Delimont — 56 (middle)

INDEX

Page numbers in boldface type indicate illustrations

TO FIND OUT MORE

BOOKS

Armbruster, Ann. *St. Lawrence Seaway*. New York: Children's Press, 1996.

Bliss, Johathan. *The Stanley Cup*. Vero Beach, Fla.: Rourke Book Company, Inc., 1994.

Carpenter, Donna Gibbs. *Daytripper 2: 50 Trips In and Around Toronto*. Toronto: Boston Mills Press, 1992.

Coulter, Tony. *Jacques Cartier, Samuel de Champlain, and the Explorers of Canada*. New York: Chelsea House Publishers, 1993.

Goodman, Michael E. *Toronto Raptors*. Mankato, Minn.: Creative Education, 1998.

Gould, Allan. *Fodor's Toronto*. New York: Fodor's Travel Publications, Inc., 1991.

Goyens, Chrys. *Montreal Maple Leafs*. Mankato, Minn.: Creative Education, 1994.

Grabowski, John F. *Canada*. Modern Nations of the World series. San Diego: Lucent Books, 1998.

Kasher, Robert. *Passport's Guide to Ethnic Toronto: A Complete Guide to the Many Faces and Cultures of Toronto*. Champlain, N.Y.: Passport Books, 1997.

LeVert, Suzanne. *Let's Discover Canada: Ontario*. New York: Chelsea House, 1992.

Murphy, Jack and Wendy Murphy. *Toronto*. Great Cities series. New York: Rosen Publishing, 1992.

Rambeck, Richard. *The History of the Toronto Blue Jays*. Mankato, Minn.: Creative Education, 1999.

ONLINE SITES

CN Tower:
www.cntower.ca
All you want to know about Toronto's best-known landmark, the tallest free-standing tower in the world from which visitors have a beautiful view of the entire city; includes links to hours, location, and rates; space-age games and attractions; restaurants (including the elegant revolving 360 Restaurant at the top of the tower); shopping at the Marketplace; fascinating facts; and more.

Heritage Toronto
www.torontohistory.on.ca
This site has links called History Comes Alive (a tour, with a map, of Toronto's museums including Fort York, The Pier, Colborne Lodge—a restored 1830s Regency-style cottage—and more); Special Events, month-by-month throughout the year; Teaching Toronto (information on museum programs and tools for teachers, including a Toronto history quiz); and more.

Toronto Maple Leafs:
www.torontomapleleafs.com
The Toronto Maple Leafs professional hockey team home page has links to the players, stats, schedule, history, gift store, and more.

Visiting Toronto:
www.tourism-toronto.com
Includes information on live music, shopping, restaurants, sports and leisure, hotels, arts and entertainment, and much more.

ABOUT THE AUTHORS

Stillman (Tim) and Barbara Rogers have written guidebooks to Canada for Thomas Cook Publishing in London and for Frommer's Guides. Most recently, they wrote the 646-page *Adventure Guide to Canada's Atlantic Provinces*. Stillman is the author of *Montreal* in the Cities of the World series and together they wrote *Canada* in the Enchantment of the World series, both published by Children's Press. Barbara and their daughter Lura are co-authors of *Dominican Republic*, in the Enchantment of the World Series. Stillman and Barbara are the authors of books on South Africa, Zambia, and Peru, for the Children of the World series.